DANCE

by Karen Marie Graves

Consultant:
Heidi L. Schimpf, Director of Education and Outreach
Joy of Motion Dance Center, Washington, D.C.

Capstone

Mankato, Minnesota

Snap Books are published by Capstone Press,
151 Good Counsel Drive, P.O. Box 669, Mankato, Minnesota 56002.
www.capstonepress.com

Library of Congress Cataloging-in-Publication Data
Graves, Karen Marie.
    Tap dancing / by Karen Marie Graves.
    p. cm.—(Snap books. Dance)
    Summary: "Describes tap dance, including history, training, moves, and
performance"—Provided by publisher.
    Includes bibliographical references and index.
    ISBN-13: 978-1-4296-0124-5 (hardcover)
    ISBN-10: 1-4296-0124-8 (hardcover)
    1. Tap dancing—Juvenile literature. 2. Tap dancing. I. Title. II. Series.
GV1794.G729 2008
792.7'8—dc22   2007005398

Editor: Megan Schoeneberger

Designer: Veronica Bianchini

Photo Researchers: Charlene Deyle and Wanda Winch

Photo Credits:
AP Photo/Kathy Willens, 9; Capstone Press/Karon Dubke, cover, 2–3, 5, 6, 11, 13, 15, 16, 17 (all), 18, 19 (all), 20,
21, 22, 23, 25, 27; Corbis/Bettmann, 7; Courtesy author Karen Graves, 32; Library of Congress, 8; Photodisc, 12;
proofsheet.com/Michal Daniel, 29

Capstone Press thanks Mitzi Roberts and the students of Dance Express, Mankato, Minnesota.

1 2 3 4 5 6 12 11 10 09 08 07

Table of Contents

Chapter One

Musical Feet

Ziggety-bop! Tap dancing is all about sound.

Put on a pair of tap shoes, and you can make music with your feet. You can pound out beats like a drummer in a band. Brush a toe across the floor, and then jump up and land with a smack. Every crash, click, and scrape adds to the rhythm of the dance.

Tap dancers mix movement and sound to express emotions. Tapping can be laid-back, with the light, graceful style of classic film dancers like Gene Kelly or Ginger Rogers. It can be quick and precise, like Irish step dancing. Or tapping can be an aggressive, loud mix of jazz and hip-hop.

Whatever the style, recent Broadway shows have brought tap dancing back to a new generation. Are you ready to tap your way into the spotlight?

An American Art Form

Tap dance was born in the American colonies. It began in the 1700s, when slaves watched and copied their owners' jigs and clog dances. The slaves then mixed that fast footwork with their own African rhythms and steps. The result was an early form of tap dance.

After 1910, metal pieces called taps were made specially to fit dancers' shoes. It was then that tap dancing earned its name.

Tap dance passed from generation to generation like a story. On street corners, in clubs, or in traveling shows, dancers often faced off in tap dance challenges. In a challenge, dancers took turns trying to out-tap each other. The audience's boos or cheers determined who was the better dancer. Each time a dancer copied, shared, stole, or added on to another's moves, tap dance grew and changed.

The Nicholas Brothers, 1941

Tapping through Time:
A Brief Look at the History of Tap Dancing

History means a lot to tap dancers. Today's tappers get their inspiration from the long line of tap masters who danced before them. In this way, dancers are loyal to the past, even while making up their own steps and styles.

1910
Dancers begin adding metal taps to their shoes.

1928
Blackbirds of 1928 **opens on Broadway, making Bill "Bojangles" Robinson an early tap star.**

Bill Robinson

1935
Films carry tap dancing from the Broadway stage to the big screen. Shirley Temple dances with Bill Robinson in *The Little Colonel.*

1956
Elvis Presley releases one of the first rock 'n' roll records. As new rock 'n' roll dances are created, tap dancing fades out of style.

In the Spotlight:
Savion Glover

Dancer and choreographer Savion Glover is one of today's tap masters. At age 23, he choreographed and starred in the hit musical *Bring in 'da Noise, Bring in 'da Funk*. Audiences loved Glover's fresh, edgy style called "power-tapping" or "hitting." It borrows energy, sound, and rhythm from rap and hip-hop music. By mixing old and new, Glover has kept tap dancing alive for a whole new generation of dancers and fans.

1975
Tap dancing makes a comeback when *The Wiz* **opens** on Broadway.

1996
Broadway's *Bring in 'da Noise, Bring in 'da Funk* **opens.** Powerful, edgy rhythm tap becomes popular.

Savion Glover

2005
Savion Glover debuts *Classical Savion*, which pairs classical music with modern tap dancing.

Class Act

Tap dancing isn't exactly simple, but you don't need a lot of classes before you can shuffle-hop-step your way through a pretty cool routine.

Compare that to ballet, where it's a safe guess that you won't be doing any pirouettes by the end of your first or even fifth lesson.

This book will give you a head start, but to learn tap, you're going to need to see and hear the steps. That means you'll need to find a good class. Look in the phone book or online for a studio.

Then check it out with an adult. If you can, peek in on a class.

Take a good look at the studio's floors. They should be wood, not concrete. Concrete can wreck your shoes and cause serious injury. Large mirrors on the studio's wall should allow students to see themselves and their teacher during class.

Gearing Up

Try to get your tap shoes in time for the first class. Track them down at stores that sell dance supplies. The shoes should fit snugly but comfortably. Oxfords with low, broad heels are the easiest to dance in. The taps are bigger too, so they make the best sounds. Taps are sometimes sold separately from the shoes. Just have them screwed on at a shoe repair shop. Once the taps are on, you're good to go.

While you're learning the footwork, wear whatever is comfortable. Just make sure it is something you can sweat in. When you take more advanced classes that focus on arms, line, and style, you might want something close-fitting, like a leotard and tights.

1.3

Nuts and Bolts

Learning to tap dance is like building with blocks.

You start with the simplest single sound—one tap striking the floor. Then you move on to two sounds, like a shuffle or a flap. These basics make up the foundation of tap dance.

As you learn, you add to the number of sounds. Each new sound is a block. Put the blocks together, and you're building steps. In no time, you'll be amazed at the music your feet are making.

Single Sounds

Even the best tap dancers had to start with the easy stuff. Break in your tap shoes by learning to make these basic sounds.

STEP

The first step to learn is just that—a step! Keep your weight off your heels when you step.

- Pick your right foot up from the floor.

- Step down, changing your weight completely onto the ball of your right foot.

HOP

A hop is also as simple as it sounds—just hop!

- Stand with your weight on your right foot.

- Jump up and land on your right foot.

BRUSH

A brush is a kicking movement. It makes a single sound.

- Lift your right foot.

- Swing it forward, brushing only your toe tap on the floor as though you are kicking something out of the way.

- To do a back brush, swing your foot back, brushing your toe tap on the floor.

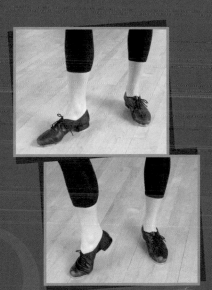

Double Up

Now build on those brushes and steps. Mix them to add a second sound.

Tip!

Keep your knees slightly bent when you dance to beat out the steps loudly and clearly.

FLAP (da-DUH)

Flaps are often used to tap across the stage.
They can be done forward or backward.

- Brush with your right foot, using the toe tap only.

- Step onto the ball of your right foot.

SHUFFLE (da-DUH)

Shuffles are a combination of two brushes.

- Brush your right foot forward using the toe tap only.

- Brush back with your right foot. Emphasize the beat on the brush back.

BALL CHANGE (DUH-DUH)

A ball change can be done forward, to the side, or in place.

- Step onto the ball of your right foot.

- Step completely onto the ball of your left foot with an even rhythm.

19

Chapter Four

Taking the Next Step

The basics you learned in the last chapter are your foundation. Learn them well, so you have a strong base to build on. Then just keep adding sounds and making new beats and rhythms with each step.

Shuffle Ball Change

Shuffle Ball Change is a combination of a shuffle and a ball change. You should hear four separate sounds, accented like this: shuff-LE BALL CHANGE.

1. Forward brush with your right foot.

2. Backward brush with your right foot.

3. Shift weight to your right foot.

4. Shift weight to your left foot.

Irish

Now let's try a step called an Irish. It looks like a simple Irish jig. It's a shuffle, a hop, and a step. Again, you should hear four sounds—shuff-LE HOP STEP.

1. Forward brush with your right foot.

2. Backward brush with your right foot.

3. Hop on your left foot.

4. Step down on your right foot.

Putting It Together

After you've practiced the steps a few times, you're ready to put them together. Here is the rhythm:

shuff-LE HOP STEP

shuff-LE HOP STEP

shuff-LE BALL CHANGE.

Try clapping it a few times so you are familiar with it. Pay attention to the stressed and unstressed sounds. Like jazz musicians, tap dancers use syncopated rhythms that stress unexpected or irregular beats.

1. Forward brush with your right foot: shuff

2. Backward brush with your right foot: LE

3. Hop on your left foot: HOP

4. Step down on your right foot: STEP

5. Forward brush with your left foot: shuff

6. Backward brush with your left foot: LE

7. Hop on your right foot: HOP

8. Step down on your left foot: STEP

9. Forward brush with your right foot: shuff

10. Backward brush with your right foot: LE

11. Shift weight to your right foot: BALL

12. Shift weight to your left foot: CHANGE

Chapter Five

Stepping Up

If you eat, breathe, and dream about tap dancing, you might be thinking about going pro. Being paid to do something you love is cool, but getting to that level means years of hard work.

Take tons of classes and do some serious practicing between every class. A one-on-one class is expensive, but you'll get training built around exactly what you need to work on. Also, once in a while a studio offers a master class. Sign up. Don't worry—you don't need to be a master. It just means that a professional dancer will teach the class. Many master classes are open to total beginners.

When you are ready, you'll find a range of pro jobs you can do. Regional theaters often need dancers for musical productions. It's a great way to build up your experience.

Traveling tap dance companies like the National Tap Ensemble or Tap Manhattan perform across the country and around the world. Joining a company is an opportunity to work with and learn from many talented performers. And finally, making it big on Broadway will take tons of experience and lots of competitive auditions.

And the Beat
Goes On

Learning to tap dance takes patience, determination,

and lots of practice. But if you stick with it, in time

you'll be electrifying audiences with all sorts

of earth-shaking steps!

Glossary

ball (BAWL)—the cushioned part of the foot between the toes and the arch

beat (BEET)—the steady pulse of sounds in music and drumming

choreographer (kor-ee-OG-ruh-fur)—a person who arranges dance steps

rhythm (RITH-uhm)—the way stressed and unstressed beats are put together to make a pattern

syncopated (sing-kuh-PAY-ted)—having a rhythm in which stress is placed on unexpected or irregular beats

Fast Facts

Before 1910, tap dancing was known as jigging or buck dancing.

Be sure to wear your dancing shoes every May 25. Not only is it the birthday of early tap star Bill "Bojangles" Robinson, but it is also National Tap Dance Day.

In the 1940s, tap dancer Ann Miller starred in many Hollywood musicals. She was known as the fastest female tap dancer in the world. Some people believed she could dance 500 taps per minute.

Read More

Cutcher, Jenai. *Gotta Dance!: The Rhythms of Jazz and Tap.* The Curtain Call Library of Dance. New York: Rosen, 2004.

Glover, Savion, and Bruce Weber. *Savion!: My Life in Tap.* New York: W. Morrow and Co., 2000.

Hasday, Judy L. *Savion Glover: Entertainer.* Black Americans of Achievement, Legacy Edition. New York: Chelsea House, 2006.

Hebach, Susan. *Tap Dancing.* After School High Interest Books. New York: Children's Press, 2001.

Internet Sites

FactHound offers a safe, fun way to find Internet sites related to this book. All of the sites on FactHound have been researched by our staff.

Here's how:

1. Visit *www.facthound.com*

2. Choose your grade level.

3. Type in this book ID **1429601248** for age-appropriate sites. You may also browse subjects by clicking on letters, or by clicking on pictures and words.

4. Click on the **Fetch It** button.

Facthound will fetch the best sites for you!

About the Author

Karen Marie Graves started dance lessons at 9 and performed semi-professionally through middle and high school. While a student at the University of California, Los Angeles, she paid for her classes by teaching dance. After graduation, she continued teaching and began writing part time. She was Dance Director of the children's department at a studio in Westwood and taught ballet, tap, and jazz dance for 20 years before becoming a full-time writer.

INDEX